ב"ה

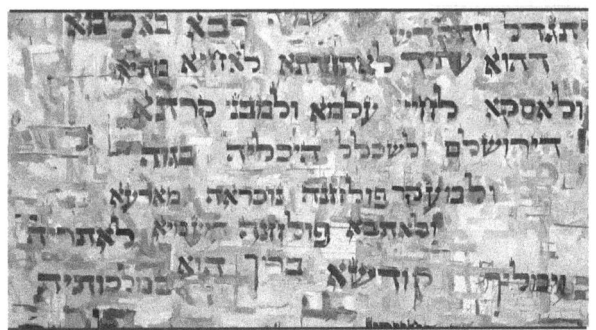

UNDERSTANDING THE MOURNER'S KADDISH

THE MYSTERY OF KADDISH

לעלוי נשמת מרת רחל בת אברהם נ"ע

RABBI DOVBER PINSON

IYYUN PUBLISHING

THE MYSTERY OF KADDISH © 2012 Dovber Pinson.
All rights reserved. No part of this book may be used or reproduced in any manner whatsoever without written permission except in the case of brief quotations embodied in critical articles and reviews.

Published by IYYUN Publishing
232 Bergen Street
Brooklyn, NY 11217

http:/www.IYYUN.com

Iyyun Publishing books may be purchased for educational, business or sales promotional use. For information please contact: contact@IYYUN.com

cover image: David Baruch Wolk
cover and book design: Rochie Pinson

pb ISBN 978-0-9852011-0-4
Pinson, DovBer 1971-
The Mystery of Kaddish: Understanding the Mourner's Kaddish/ DovBer Pinson

1. Judaism 2. Spirituality 3. Self-help

'THE MYSTERY OF KADDISH'
was prepared in honor and in loving memory
of my dear Mother,

ROCHEL BAS AVRAHAM ז"ל
מרת רחל בת אברהם ז"ל

for the day of her *Sh'loshim*,
the 11th day of Teves,
which is the Tenth month of the year.

Teves contains the word *Tov*, 'good'. 'Ten' is the number of
Kedusha which sweetens the paradigm of 'eleven' —
and this is also the power of Kaddish.

The day of the Petirah was on
יום ד' פ' וישלח י"ב כסלו התשע"ב
Which has the same numerical value as her name
רחל בת אברהם ושרה

With deep gratitude,
RAV DOVBER PINSON

Rosh Yeshivah IYYUN
IYYUN: Center for Jewish Spirituality
www.IYYUN.com

נגדל ויתקדש
דהוא עתיד לאתחדתא
לאסקא לחיי עלמא ולמב[נא]
דירושלם ולשכלל היכלי[ה]
ולמעקר פולחנה [נוכראה]
ולאתבא פולחנא
קודשא בריך
ויבדרון ביומיכון וב[יומי]
ישראל בעגלא וביומן ק[ריב]
לאתחדתא לאחזאה ב[תיא]
עלמא ולמבני קרתא
לשכלל היכליה בגוה
פולחנה נוכראה מארעא

TABLE OF CONTENTS

TRANSLATION & TRANSLITERATION
OF THE MOURNER'S KADDISH 1

I: WHY KADDISH? 3

II: A HISTORICAL PERSPECTIVE 7

III: JOURNEY TO THE GARDEN OF EDEN 10

IV: INTERPRETATIONS WITHIN THE TEXT
OF KADDISH 12

V: AMEIN 32

A TRANSLATION & TRANSLITERATION OF THE

MOURNER'S KADDISH

May the Great Name be exalted and sanctified

In the world that was created according to His will
And may His Kingdom be established
And may redemption sprout forth
And may His anointed one come soon.

May it happen in your lifetime
And in your days
And in the lifetime of all the House of Israel
Speedily and very soon,
And they should say Amein

May His great name be blessed forever and for all eternity!

Blessed, lauded, beautified,
exalted, raised up, glorified,
elevated and praised,
be the name of the Holy One, blessed be He
Higher than any blessing, song,
praise or consolation
that we could say in the world,
And they should say Amein

May there be abundant peace from Heaven,
and a good life, for us and for all Israel,
And say, Amein.

He Who makes peace in His exalted realms,
may He make peace for us and for all Israel,
And say, Amein.

Yis-gadal v'yis-kadash sh'may rabo.	יִתְגַּדַּל וְיִתְקַדַּשׁ שְׁמֵהּ רַבָּא
(Cong. Omayn)	אמן

B'ol'mo di v'ro chir'u-say	בְּעָלְמָא דִּי בְרָא כִרְעוּתֵהּ
v'yam-lich mal'chusay, v'yatz-mach	וְיַמְלִיךְ מַלְכוּתֵהּ, וְיַצְמַח
pur-konay viko-rayv m'shi-chay.	פֻּרְקָנֵהּ וִיקָרֵב מְשִׁיחֵהּ
(Cong. Omayn)	אמן

B'cha-yay-chon uv'yomay-chon	בְּחַיֵּיכוֹן וּבְיוֹמֵיכוֹן
uv'cha-yay d'chol bays yisro-ayl,	וּבְחַיֵּי דְכָל בֵּית יִשְׂרָאֵל,
ba-agolo uviz'man koriv	בַּעֲגָלָא וּבִזְמַן קָרִיב
v'im'ru omayn. (Cong. Omayn Y'hay	וְאִמְרוּ אָמֵן: אמן. יְהֵא שְׁמֵהּ
sh'may rabo m'vorach l'olam ul'ol'may	רַבָּא מְבָרַךְ לְעָלַם וּלְעָלְמֵי
ol'ma-yo. Yisboraych)	עָלְמַיָּא: יִתְבָּרַךְ

Y'hay sh'may rabo m'vorach	יְהֵא שְׁמֵהּ רַבָּא מְבָרַךְ
l'olam ul'ol'may ol'ma-yo.	לְעָלַם וּלְעָלְמֵי עָלְמַיָּא
Yis-boraych, v'yish-tabach,	יִתְבָּרַךְ וְיִשְׁתַּבַּח,
v'yispo-ayr, v'yis-romom,	וְיִתְפָּאַר, וְיִתְרוֹמַם,
v'yis-nasay, v'yis-hador,	וְיִתְנַשֵּׂא, וְיִתְהַדָּר,
v'yis-aleh, v'yis-halol, sh'may	וְיִתְעַלֶּה, וְיִתְהַלָּל, שְׁמֵהּ
d'kud-sho b'rich hu.	דְּקֻדְשָׁא בְּרִיךְ הוּא
(Cong. Omayn)	אמן

L'aylo min kol bir'choso v'shi-roso,	לְעֵלָּא מִן כָּל בִּרְכָתָא וְשִׁירָתָא,
tush-b'choso v'neche-moso,	תֻּשְׁבְּחָתָא וְנֶחֱמָתָא,
da-amiron b'ol'mo,	דַּאֲמִירָן בְּעָלְמָא,
v'im'ru omayn.	וְאִמְרוּ אָמֵן
(Cong. Omayn)	אמן

Y'hay sh'lomo rabo min sh'ma-yo,	יְהֵא שְׁלָמָא רַבָּא מִן שְׁמַיָּא
v'cha-yim tovim olay-nu v'al kol	וְחַיִּים טוֹבִים עָלֵינוּ וְעַל כָּל
yisro-ayl v'im'ru omayn.	יִשְׂרָאֵל וְאִמְרוּ אָמֵן
(Cong. Omayn)	אמן

Take three steps back and say the following, while bowing the head to the right, straight ahead, left, straight ahead, and bowing down (as indicated):

> Oseh sholom bim'romov, ^ hu	> עֹשֶׂה שָׁלוֹם בִּמְרוֹמָיו, ^ הוּא
< ya-aseh sholom olaynu, ^ v'al kol	> יַעֲשֶׂה שָׁלוֹם עָלֵינוּ, ^ וְעַל כָּל
yisro-ayl, v'im'ru omayn.	יִשְׂרָאֵל, וְאִמְרוּ אָמֵן
(Cong. Omayn)	אמן

CHAPTER I:
WHY KADDISH?

Reciting *Kaddish* is universally practiced to honor or merit a person who has passed on. It is curious that this particular prayer became the deifinitive symbol of mourning. There are certainly many other powerful ways to commemorate and honor the beloved deceased, which have been offered to us by our Sages, and have been sustained as a practice for many centuries. Some of these are;

• Charity: There are many sources that speak of the great soul-elevation accomplished through giving charity in honor of a deceased person.*[1]*

• Mausoleum: Some sources speak about building a mausoleum.*[2]*

- Gravestone: Erecting a gravestone or monument creates a seat for the makifim or transcendent levels of the person's soul. In the Gemara, the headstone is referred to as the nefesh, since this level of soul permeates it.*[3]*

- Torah Study: One should study Torah in honor of the deceased.*[4]*

- Haftorah: One should recite the Haftorah in the merit of a deceased parent.*[5]*

- Lighting a Candle: Lighting a candle during the Shiva period creates joy for the soul. In general, souls receive pleasure when we light candles in their memory. There is an established custom to light a candle every year on the date of a person's passing.*[6]*

Yet, with all these meaningful traditions at hand, Kaddish still stands out as the definitive practice of mourning among all these forms of commemoration.

Why is this? Furthermore, what do the ancient Aramaic words of Kaddish really mean to express?

Lamentation for the dead? Comfort for the living? A declaration of faith in Hashem in the face of difficult losses?

Kaddish speaks of exalting the "Great Name" of Hashem, our Creator. What does this have to do with commemorating the departed? Why pray to exalt the Great Name when someone dies? How might this bring solace to the living, or assistance for the soul of the departed?

If Kaddish is meant to help the living reaffirm their belief in Divine justice, then perhaps it should say, "I humbly accept upon myself the judgment of Hashem." From the wording of the Kaddish it seems rather that it is more a statement of continuation and determination; despite their loss, the living pledge that they will continue their beloved's work in sanctifying Hashem's name in this world.

Before we begin exploring the Kaddish in more depth, let us clarify that there are various forms of Kaddish, the primary ones being the *Chatzi Kaddish* or 'Half Kaddish' and the *Kaddish Shaleim*, or 'Full Kaddish'. During the actual prayers, we most frequently use the Half Kaddish, which marks a transition within the daily prayer service. Another form is the *Kaddish d'Rabbanan*, the 'Kaddish of the Sages', which is recited after a group of people has studied Torah. The version we are discussing is 'Mourner's Kaddish', otherwise known as *Kaddish Yasom*, literally, the 'Orphan's Kaddish'.

CHAPTER II:
A HISTORICAL PERSPECTIVE

The core of the Kaddish prayer dates back to the period after the destruction of the first Temple, and was established by the Members of the Great Assembly *(Aruch HaShulchan, 55:1)*. It was composed in Aramaic, the ancient language that all the Jews spoke during the period after the destruction of the Temple, so that everyone could understand the meaning of the words *(Tosefos on Berachos, 3a)* including non-Jews *(Kol Bo, 7)*.

This shows that in our times, those hearing Kaddish, and certainly those reciting it, should understand the meaning of the words.

The oldest known version of the Mourner's Kaddish is found in the oldest known prayer book, the Siddur of Rav Amram Gaon of the 9th Century, C.E. While it is clear that Kaddish has been a universal practice for hundreds of years, it is uncertain at what point it became common practice to recite Kaddish for a person who passed on.

The idea of saying a prayer to spiritually assist someone who passed on has a source in Tanach: King David prayed for his late son, Avshalom *(Sh'muel II, 19:1; Sotah, 10b)*. A story in the Gemara mentions the importance of specifically reciting Kaddish for the deceased:[9]

> *Rabbi Akiva said that once he was walking on the road and encountered a man covered in coal dust, carrying a heavy load of wood that he had collected. Rabbi Akiva greeted him and inquired, "Are you a slave? If so, perhaps I can redeem you. Or, are you destitute? If so, I could give you some money." The man replied that he was neither a slave nor poor. "Rebbe, I am dead, not alive!" The man explained that this was part of his afterlife soul-journey; he needed to rectify and achieve a tikkun for actions done during his life, and he was experiencing the energy of harsh judgment.*

> *Rabbi Akiva asked him if his 'supervisors', as it were, had indicated any way that he could be unburdened from this hardship. The man answered, "I heard it said, that if I had a son who would stand amid the congregation and say Kaddish, and if the congregation would respond, 'May the Great Name be blessed,' I would be released from this suffering."*
>
> *Rabbi Akiva asked him where he lived during his life. He went there and found one of the man's sons, circumcised him, taught him Torah, and eventually this person was able to say Kaddish and Barchu. The father was then released from his torment.*
>
> *Later on, this man came to Rabbi Akiva in a dream and said that he was now in Gan Eden.*

We can see from this story that the principle of Kaddish is that "A child can bring merit to a parent" *(Sanhedrin, 104a).* On a deeper level, parents and children share a common soul-root within the great, primordial soul of Adam—our actions below have an impact in Heaven and an impact upon other souls that are connected to us. Thus, over time, it became a common custom for one to recite Kaddish for deceased parents—to help, if needed, expedite their journeys into Gan Eden *(Rama, Siman 376:6).*

CHAPTER III:
JOURNEY TO THE GARDEN OF EDEN

Eventually, all souls get to Gan Eden. Any experience of torment along the way is not meant as a 'punishment', rather as a sponge that soaks up all negativity, so that the soul, or the 'memory', can survive in Gan Eden.*[7]*

A bodiless soul can no longer achieve elevation. It has passed into a world of pure spiritual being-ness, where there is no more opportunity for 'doing'. At that point, only living persons connected with this departed soul on the physical plane (which indicates a spiritual connection or common root-soul in higher planes), can help the departed gain spiritual movement.

Kaddish, from this perspective, is a negation of negativity, a removal of torment, or a way of helping a soul who is stuck. The Arizal teaches that there is also a positive reason for reciting Kaddish. It is to help souls ascend into higher, deeper levels of Gan Eden: "The purpose of Kaddish is not only to assist a soul in gaining release from the judgment of Gehenom, as is commonly believed, it is also to assist a soul that is already within Gan Eden to rise higher and higher" *(Sha'ar HaKavannos, Derush Kaddish)*. Therefore, Kaddish is beneficial even to Tzadikim.

Kaddish is also beneficial to the living who recite it; the activity of exalting and sanctifying the Name is a healing practice. Reciting Kaddish among other mourners helps create fellowship where each person helps the others mitigate feelings of loneliness or hopelessness. In the face of despair, we create a small community of healing and recommitting ourselves to sanctifying Hashem's name.

CHAPTER IV:

INTERPRETATIONS WITHIN THE TEXT OF KADDISH

Yisgadal V'Yiskadash Shmeih Rabbah
'May the Great name be exalted and sanctified'

Kaddish begins with the words *Yisgadal v'yiskadash shmeih raba,* 'May the Great Name be exalted and sanctified.' What 'Great Name' is this, and why is it not already exalted? Why pray to exalt the Great Name when someone dies? How might this bring solace to the living, or assistance for the soul of the departed?

One simple, inner meaning of the phrase *Shmeih Raba* or 'the Great Name', is 'the Divine Name that creates everything'; *raba*, 'great', has the same letters as *Bara*, 'Creator'. When a death—a concealing of life—is experienced, the Creator's Name is also concealed from perception *(Avudraham)*. One inner meaning of the word *Mevarach* (from *Baruch*) is 'reveal'. Therefore, when we say *Y'hei Sh'mei Rabba Mevarach...*, we are saying, "May the Name of the Creator be revealed, forever, and for all eternity."

We are the "limbs of the *Shechina*" *(Magid of Mezritch)*. The pain we suffer here below, causes the Divine Presence to 'experience pain' as well: "*Imo Anochi b'tzarah*," "I am with him in suffering."

When we are in exile, the Shechinah is in exile *(Megilah, 29a)*. Since our soul is a part of Hashem, the agony that the soul experiences in *Galus* or 'exile'—physical and spiritual limitation—also causes a type of Galus or confinement, for the Presence of Hashem on earth. "The human soul is Hashem's candle" *(Mishlei, 20:27)*. When there is a diminishing of 'Hashem's candle' on earth, there is a lessening of Divine energy, so to speak, within Creation.

When a person passes on, he takes away part of Hashem's light in the world, and thus Hashem's presence is felt less.

This may be illustrated by a scenario in 16th Century Europe, when suicide began to be widely outlawed. The taking of ones life was seen as an offence against the local king; death meant one less subject, and this diminished the king's grandeur. Similarly, every human being is made in the Divine image, and everyone is precious. Imagine a coin bearing the image of the king. If the coin were to be lost, the 'image' of the king would be diminished in the world. When a person passes on, Hashem's image is less apparent in this world.

Kaddish, which we would expect to mention the deceased and the journey of the deceased's soul in the afterlife, instead speaks only of the Creator's glory. Since when one person leaves this world there is one less player in the orchestra of the Master of the Universe, we therefore sanctify and glorify Hashem's name; we affirm and replenish Hashem's Presence in the world through the mitzvah of Kaddish. Thus, the function of Kaddish is to comfort the Divine Presence, as it were.

This is also why we recite Kaddish in Aramaic, a 'secular language'.*[8]* Speaking a more worldly language helps us draw down Hashem's Presence into our mundane world, and into a world of separation, death, and pain. The Divine Presence in the world becomes whole again.

The word Kaddish has a numerical value of 414: Kuf (100), Dalet (4), Yud (10), Shin (300). This number is two times 207, and 207 is the value of the word ohr, 'light'. 'Double light' alludes to the simultaneous presence of the *Ohr Yashar*, 'Direct Light', explicit or apparent light and joy, and the *Ohr Chozer*, 'Reflected Light', light that emerges from within darkness or sadness. By means of Kaddish, we pray that we should have both forms of light: we should have the light that emerges out of our mourning process, 'Reflected Light'—but from now on, we should have only direct, revealed light in our lives.

In the experience of the death of a loved one, there is a muting of the divine energy or light in one's life. Some people begin to focus on painful questions such as, 'Why did this happen? What was the Divine purpose in it? Why me? Why now?' It seems there are no answers, and nothing to say. Because this muting is an organic part of the mourning process, mourners are advised: *Ha'anek dom*, 'remain silent' *(Moed Katan, 15a)*. Since they are, during this time, 'separate from the light', they are like a silent, empty 'vessel'. A mourner is considered an *Ilem*, a 'mute' person.

The Divine name *Elokim* alludes to constriction and limitation, such as is experienced in a condition of mourning. The letters in Elokim can spell out the phrase *Ilem Yud-Hei*, 'the Yud-Hei is muted' or the supernal Light of Yud-Hei is not visible. In other words, in a full grieving process, there is a separation between the higher part of the name of Hashem (Yud-Hei) and the lower part (Vav-Hei). The numerical value of Vav (6) and Hei (5) is 11. When Vav-Hei falls away from Yud-Hei, and becomes isolated, the energy of 'eleven' stands out—eleven being associated with *Kelipa*, 'covering' or husk of concealment. When Vav-Hei is covered with Kelipa, the Light of Yud-Hei above becomes obscured from perception.

The number ten represents wholeness or perfection. There are ten *sefiros* or vessels designed to receive the One Light. When the vessels receive the Light and allow it to unify with them, the result is ten luminous *sefiros*. When the Light is not allowed to unify with the vessels, the light and vessels retain their separate identities and there is one Light plus ten vessels, adding up to eleven separate elements. The energy of Divine Light is then muted and cannot express itself directly in the world. Kelipa results.

On a practical level, Kelipa implies negativity, because negativity seems to conceal the positive nature of the Infinite Light. When we experience something as positive, whatever it may be, while we may not recognize it consciously, we are filled with light, joy, meaning or purpose. Conversely, when confronted with tragedy or death, we experience darkness, a concealing of light and joy. When we are suffering, we may not sense the reason or wisdom behind the events in our lives.

Every experience has both a 'light' and a 'vessel': the experience itself is the vessel, whereas its meaning or purpose is the light. A vessel without light is Kelipa.

In our daily lives, we are capable of both 'Kelipa-perception' and 'non-Kelipa perception'. At times, we perceive the Light or the 'Hand of the Creator' guiding us; at other times all we can perceive is the apparently random, external dimension of life, a vessel without the Light of the Divine Presence.

The meta-cause of death, separation and Kelipa, is the fragmentation within the Name of Hashem, the split between the Vav-Hei and the Yud-Hei. When there is a division within this 'source', division and death manifest in the world.

In our historical era, the Great Name, the Yud-Hei-Vav-Hei, is still generally divided by the force called *Amalek (Shemos, 17:16)*. Amalek represents the Kelipa of spiritual coldness, doubt, and the separation between the mind and heart. We pray that the Divine Name should become complete and whole again *(Machzor Vitri; See B'rachos, 3a, Tosefos, ad loc)*. However, our sages also say, "Hashem vowed that His Name…will not be complete until Amalek's name is totally obliterated" *(Tanchuma, Ki Setzei, 11; Rashi, ibid)*. How is Amalek's name, and his Kelipa, wiped out?

The words *Yisgadal Ve'yiskadash* contain eleven Hebrew letters and thus correspond to the Vav-Hei (11). The letters of the word *Shmeih* spell out *Sheim* Yud-Hei, 'the Divine Name Yud-Hei'. *Yisgadal v'yiskadash shmeih raba* therefore means that the Vav-Hei should be elevated to and reunited with the Yud-Hei; may the Divine energy isolated in the lower realms rise, and become one with the Light of the *Shmeih*, the Name Yud-Hei. When they are in oneness, Yud-Hei and Vav-Hei will then be *Rabah*, 'great' or complete. When the Vav-Hei is thus elevated and sanctified, the negative power of 'eleven', Kelipa, or the influence of Amalek, is wiped out, and only the greater unity of the Divine Name remains. The 'vessel' is integrated with the 'light'; experience and meaning are aligned in our lives.

[* Another, similar way of looking at this is that *Shmeih Rabah* has seven letters, alluding to *Kedusha*, holiness. Therefore, we're praying that the Divine spark in Vav-Hei rise and become unified in its source in holiness, the Yud-hei.]

When this great alignment is activated, even when we experience emotional and spiritual contraction, or the power of 'Elokim', that very experience becomes transparent to the Yud-Hei. The condition of 'Ilem' opens, and we can see through the events of our lives to the Great Name.

Then, even in our grief, we are one with the Light. This brings us deep healing, and it contributes to the healing of the entire world.

The numerical value of the word *Shmeih*, 'Name', is 345, the same as the value of *E-l Shad-dai*, one of the seven sacred names of Hashem. On the other hand, 345 is also equivalent to the words *Elokim Acheirim* 'foreign deities' or forces of alienation. When we observe the light of the sacred names of Hashem in everything, all forces of alienation and separation in the universe are nullified; the Shmeih becomes Rabah, great.

Yisgadal v'yiskadash shmeih rabah: these four words correspond to the four letters in the name of Hashem: Yud, Hei, Vav and Hei. When we 'fill' these four letters with an Aleph, the sum of the letters is 10:

Yud is spelled 'Yud-Vav-Dalet', which are 3 letters.
Hei is spelled 'Hei-Aleph', which are 2 letters.
Vav is spelled 'Vav-Aleph-Vav'. which are 3 letters.
Hei is spelled 'Hei-Aleph', which are 2 letters.

$3 + 2 + 3 + 2 = 10$

This is another illustration of the fact that when we create Kedusha or 'sanctification', the 'number ten' manifests, meaning the energy of completion and perfection.

We are sealed from the influence of the number eleven—Kelipa, separation, and negativity.

> ...Be'alma Di-V'ra Chirusei;
> v'Yamlich Malchusei, v'Yatzmach Purkanei
> v'Kareiv Meshichei
> *...In the world that was created according to His will;*
> *May His Kingdom be established, May Redemption sprout*
> *forth, and may His Anointed One come soon.*

This passage contains ten words, again signifying the energy of completion. It also alludes to the Ten Utterances of Creation and the Ten Utterances of Revelation, as will shortly be explained.

> B'Chayeichon, uv'Yomeichon, uv'Chayei
> d'Chol Beis Yisrael, Ba'Agalah u'Vizman Kariv,
> v'Imru, Amein.
> *May it happen in your lifetime, and in your days,*
> *and in the lifetime of all the House of Israel, speedily and*
> *very soon, and they should say, Amein.*

These words in the Kaddish, from *"May it happen in your lifetime…"* to *"…Amein"* form a distinct prayer in itself, and they are not part of the flow of the actual Kaddish, as the AriZal points out. This is a prayer for world redemption to come—*Ba'agalah* meaning 'suddenly' *(Rokeach)*, and *u'Vizman Kariv* meaning 'swiftly'. The words "in your lifetime" and "in your days" and "in the lifetime of all the house of Israel" are affirmations of life, of continuity in the face of death. Since an end of life has been experienced, Kaddish allows the mourner to affirm life and continuity, many times each day.

Y'hei Shmei Rabba Mevarach l'Olam ul-Almei Almaya.

May His great name be blessed forever and for all eternity.

This sentence is the essence and focus of the entire Kaddish. It is an Aramaic translation of the Hebrew phrase *Baruch sheim malchuso l'olam va'ed*, 'Blessed is the Name of His Kingdom, for ever and ever' *(Targum Yerushalmi, Devarim, 6:4)*. It is also related to a verse in Yechezkel: "I will exalt and sanctify Myself" *(38:23)*. This latter verse comes from a chapter about the battle of Gog and Magog and the future time when "Hashem's Name will be One" *(Siddur of Rabbi Yaakov Emden, M'B, Siman 56:2).*

The Gemara says that when we recite *Amein, Y'hei shmei rabah…*, the Holy One, as it were, nods His head and says: "…And what is there for a father who distances his children? And woe to the children who have been exiled from the table of their father" *(Berachos, 3a).* In other words, the recitation of Kaddish causes Hashem's compassion to be stirred for us. Hashem wants to bring all of us back together, around His great 'table'.

"When we say *Amein, Y'hei shmeih raba…* with all our *Koach* or 'strength', and with intention and raised volume *(Rashi, Tosefos, Shabbos, 119b)*, all negative decrees are annulled, and the gates of Gan Eden are opened" (*ibid*).

The word *Y'hei* is spelled Yud-Hei-Aleph. These are the three letters that can form alternate spellings ('fillings') of Hei (in other words, Hei can be spelled Hei-Yud, Hei-Hei, or Hei-Aleph). With the different numerical values resulting from these spellings, the Name of Hashem, Yud-Hei-Vav-Hei, can be 'filled' in multiple ways, with different sums: 72, 63, 45, and 52. These numbers, in Hebrew, are four mystical Divine Names, AV (72), SaG (63) MaH (45) and BaN (52), together representing the ultimate fullness of Hashem's Name.

Therefore, *Amein, y'hei shmei raba* means, 'Let it be that the y'hei—the "ultimate filling" of the Shmei—be Rabah, complete.'

When this fullness is complete, the raba, the 'greatness' of the Name, becomes a ceaseless, uninterrupted flow, like a be'er, a 'well', (raba and be'er have the same letters). When the ultimate fullness of the Name is revealed, it manifests as a source of abundance of blessings and life.

The sentence, *'Y'hei shmei raba mevarach l'olam ul-almei al-maya'* has seven words and 28 letters, corresponding to the seven words and 28 letters of the first verse in the Torah, "In the beginning, Elokim created…." The seven words of 'Y'hei shmei…' also correspond to the seven planetary influences and the seven days of the week. The Beis Yosef says that the Hebrew names of the seven planetary influences (*Shabtai* or 'Saturn', Maadim or 'Mars', and so forth) together contain 28 letters *(Orach Chaim, Siman 56)*.

The 28 letters also correspond to the days of the month. The first verse in the Torah *(Bereishis, 1:1)* has seven words, corresponding to the seven days of the week, and it has twenty-eight letters, corresponding to the days of the month *(Da'as Z'kenim)*.

This same pattern can be found with the words of revelation in the opening verse of the Ten Commandments, "And G-d spoke all these words, saying" *(Shemos, 20:1)*; here again, there are seven words and twenty-eight letters. Thus, when we say "Y'hei shmei..." we are praying that all these diverse influences in Creation, including the divisions and changes within the flow of time, should be permeated by the revealed Divine Presence.

In TaNaCh, the number 28 represents 'change'. The book of Koheles *(3:2-8)* speaks of twenty-eight seasons, in which 'there is a time for everything': "There is a time to be joyous and a time to mourn, a time to speak and a time to be quiet, etc."

Change corresponds to a sense of separation and disunity. Thus, when we recite "Y'hei shmeih...," we are healing all the change and disunity in the world, and unifying it in the Great Name of Hashem. As such, Kaddish helps heals the dramatic changes involved in our separation from our beloved departed.

The number 28, written in Hebrew letters, spells the word Koach, 'strength'. This alludes to the advice of the Gemara, quoted above, that we are to recite "Y'hei shmeih…" with all our Koach.

When Moshe went up to Heaven to receive the Torah, Hashem asked him, "Is there no *Shalom* from where you are coming?" This meant, 'Do you come from a place where people do not greet each other upon meeting?' Moshe responded, "Does a servant ever greet his master?" Hashem told him "You should have helped Me. Tell me I shall be successful." Then Moshe said, "So may the Koach of Hashem be increased, as You have said" *(Shabbos 89a; Rashi, ad loc).*

Again, the word Koach, 28, alludes to Kaddish. Therefore, Hashem was thus asking Moshe to say Kaddish, in order to increase the strength of the Divine Presence in the world, so-to-speak. Our recitation of Kaddish also 'gives strength' to Hashem.

...L'olam u-l'Almei Almaya
...Forever and for all eternity

Each of the three words in the phrase *"L'olam u–l'Almei Almaya"*, hint to the term *Olam*, 'world'. The three 'worlds' here refer the world of celestial spheres, the world of angels and the world of humans. They could also be seen as the three worlds of *B'riah* or 'Creation', *Y'tzirah* or 'Formation', and *Assiyah* or 'Completion', or the three realms of personal experience—mental, emotional and practical. When we say "L'olam u-L'almei Almaya," we are drawing down the unity of Hashem into to all of these 'worlds'. We assert that the 'Great Name' should be unified with every realm, and thus we should have direct perception of this unity within all dimensions of experience.

Yisborach, v'Yisromam...B'rich Hu
This next paragraph says:
May the name of the Holy One, blessed be He,
be blessed, lauded, beautified, exalted, raised up, glorified,
elevated and praised....'

There are eight verbs mentioned: 1) blessed, 2) lauded, 3) beautified, 4) exalted, 5) raised up, 6) glorified, 7) elevated, and 8,) praised. In the beginning of Kaddish are two verbs, "May His great name be 1) exalted, 2) and sanctified." In total there are 10 verbs, and they correspond to the Ten Expressions of the Creation of the World, such as, "Let there be light." These Ten Expressions are the outer manifestations of a deeper spiritual vibration, the *Aseres ha-Dibros*, the 'Ten Utterances' (often called 'the Ten Commandments') through which the Torah was revealed to the world.

Just as the verbs of Kaddish are grouped into a set of two and a set of eight, the Ten Utterances are subdivided into two groups: the first two that were heard by the whole community, and the latter eight that were channeled through Moshe. This correspondence shows that reciting Kaddish reveals the Unity of Hashem to the world, like the revelation of the Torah. Divine revelation creates a unity within the world as well, gently healing all the fragmentation, grief, separation, alienation, and loneliness that exist within the mourner.

In Kaddish, there are seven words beginning with the letter Vav, from *V'yishtabach, v'yispa'er, v'yishalal*: 1) and lauded 2) and beautified…7) and praised. Vav is the number six, and 7 x 6 = 42. Also, each of these seven words contains six letters, and again, 7 x 6 = 42. When we left our slavery in Egypt, it took us 42 journeys of various lengths (as elaborated in the Torah portion of Maasei), before we were able to reach our full freedom and enter the Promised Land.

The etymological root of the Hebrew word for Egypt, Mitzrayim, is metzar, 'constriction'. The 42 Journeys, according to the Baal Shem Tov, represent the 42 stages a person traverses in life toward his or her internal freedom and divine destiny. All movement, growth, elevation and internal healing demand 42 basic stages. This is reflected as well in the Kaddish. As the 42 Journeys represent the movements require to bridge one reality to the next, Kaddish is the bridge to healing after one has experienced 'separation' by means of a loved one's death. Kaddish helps the mourner journey from a place of 'desert', chaos and emptiness, toward his personal Promised Land within.

In summary, to recite Kaddish is to reveal the Unity of Hashem and the unity of all Creation, to leave one's a place of constriction, and journey toward healing and Shalom—'wholeness' and peace.

Oseh Shalom...
He Who makes peace...

The numeric value of shalom is 380: Shin (300), Lamed (30), Vav (6), Mem (40), plus 4 for the four letters themselves, equal 380. Shalom is actually a Divine Name which is the product of the Name Havayah "knocking on" the Name Ado-noi.[10] In other words, when the four letters of Havayah are placed above the four letters of Ado-noi, and multiplied vertically, they equal 380:

Yud (10)	Hei (5)	Vav (6)	Hei (5)
Aleph (1)	Dalet (4)	Nun (50)	Yud (10)
10 x 1 = 10	5 x 4 = 20	6 x 50 = 300	5 x 10 = 50

10 + 20 + 300 + 50 = 380

Real peace is when Havayah is "healed"—when there is absolute unity between Havayah, the inner reality of Hashem's Name, and Ado-noi, the outer expression of that Name.

Ado-noi is the vessel for Havayah. Today, when we are praying, we pronounce the name Havayah as Ado-noi. However, although we pronounce it this way, and in doing so we have the intention to express the meaning of the name Ado-noi, we also have the intention to express the meaning of Havayah. We have both names in mind, and thus we unite them to produce shalom.

Havayah represents the aspect of Hashem's infinity, formlessness and endlessness. Ado-noi represents the Hashem's Presence revealed within nature; Ano-noi means the 'Master'—the Master of nature, the realm of form and limitation. While Havayah is Hashem's perfect Unity, Ado-noi is Hashem's dominion over all imperfection and multiplicity, all vessels and bodies. Shalom is the unity of these two opposite paradigms.

The shalom that we are speaking of is not a 'phenomenon' or 'thing' in any ordinary sense. It's not even a blessing that emanates from Hashem. Rather it is Hashem, as it were; Shalom is a Name of Hashem (Shabbos, 10b).

When we pray that Hashem should make shalom upon us, we are therefore asking that Hashem give us Himself. The Priestly Blessing in the Torah says, "May Hashem… establish for you Shalom…and (thus) place My Name upon the children of Israel…" (Bamidbar, 6:26-27).

CHAPTER V:
AMEIN

In the Kaddish, we repeatedly say *Amein*. What does this word really mean? The common meaning is, 'May it be true,' or 'so be it.' The Talmudic sage, Rabbi Chanina, says the meaning of amein is in the acronym that it forms: *Keil Melech Ne'eman*, 'Hashem is a faithful king' *(Shabbos 119a)*.

The word Amein comes from the word Emunah, 'faith', and Emes, 'truth'. Amein is therefore a declaration of faith and truth: 'I have faith in this; I know it is true.' However, Amein is also related to the word Umnas, 'craft' or 'trade'. This teaches us that generating authentic spiritual faith and conviction requires skill and labor.

The word Amein has a 'small numeric value' of the number 10. (Aleph=1, Mem=4, Nun=5) The idea of Amein is to draw down and solidify the blessings to permeate the Ten Sefirot which correspond to the 10 utterances of creation, and thus, to the entirety of creation.

The 'full numeric value' of Amein, (91), is the same value as the word *Malach*, 'angel'. Every time we recite Amein we create holy angels, meaning, holy, positive vibrations. Amein is essentially a part of the blessing itself, and therefore when responding Amein, one should have in mind the person who said the blessing *(Rama, Siman 167:2)*. We send positive, healing energy to the mourner when we say Amein to the recitation of Kaddish.

As mentioned in the previous paragraph, the numerical value of the word Amein is 91: Aleph (1), Mem (40), Nun (50). The number ninety-one corresponds to two primary names, or manifestations, of Hashem. The value of the name *Havayah*, or the Tetragrammaton, is 26, and the Name *Ado-noi* is 65. When these two Names are united, together they equal 91 *(Me'iri, Shabbos 119b)*.

The actual Tetragrammaton, symbolized here with the

word Havayah, is ineffable—its pronunciation or vibration is 'concealed' or beyond our grasp. That is why, in prayer, when we look at the printed letters of Havayah, we only pronounce the 'revealed' name, Ado-noi. As we mentioned above, this verbal replacement creates a combination of the two names, a unification between the 'concealed', and the 'revealed'. Havayah signifies the Divine Being above, while Ado-noi, indicates the revelation and manifestation of that Being in the lower realms. By answering Amein, one brings down the blessing, that revelation from above, into the world. Therefore, "a person who answers Amein is greater than the one who says the blessing" *(Nazir, 66b)*. When we answer Amein, we unify the upper and lower Divine Names.

Because of the value of ninety-one, Amein also alludes to the *Yud-Hei*:

The spelling or 'filling' of the letter Yud is: Yud (10), Vav (6), Dalet (4) = 20. As mentioned earlier, the spelling of the letter Hei can take three forms:
Hei (5), Yud (10) = 15
Hei (5), Aleph (1) = 6
Hei (5), Hei (5) = 10.

Therefore, there are three possible numerical values for the 'filling' of the Yud-Hei:
20 + 15 = 35
20 + 6 = 26
20 + 10 = 30

When we add these three values together (35 + 26 + 30) we get a final sum of 91.

'Exalting the Great Name' means to bring the higher Light of Yud-Hei into its ultimate fullness (91), and reveal it within the 'muted' vessels of Elokim. This is the same process as uniting Havayah and Ado-noi (91). We can now understand that reciting Amein encapsulates the entire mystical purpose and function of Kaddish.

May the fallen 'eleven' of the Vav-Hei, and all fragmentation in life, be lifted into its proper unity with the Yud-Hei, thus making the Great Name complete. May this healing permeate all of creation, permanently removing all pain and grief from the entire world.

May we merit to observe the Oneness of Hashem with our own eyes, speedily and very soon, with the revealing of Mashiach, Amein.

NOTES:

[1] There are many sources that speak of the great soul-elevation accomplished through giving charity in honor of a deceased person. *Midrash, Rabbeinu Bachya, on Devarim, 21:8. Beis Yosef, Orach Chaim, 284; 621. Bach, ad loc; Tanchumah, Hazinu; Kaftor U'Perach, 44; Ramah, 621:4; Yoreh Deah, 249:16; Kav HaYashar, 86.*

[2] Some sources speak about building a mausoleum. *Yerushalmi, Shekalim, 2, 5; Sefer HaChasidim, 738.*

[3] Erecting a gravestone or monument creates a seat for the *Makifim* or transcendent levels of the person's soul. *Likutei Torah AriZal, Parshas VaYechi, p. 118; Mishnas Chassidim, Meseches Gemilus Chassadim, 3:13; Reb DovBer of Chabad: Maamor Hishtatchus, 2.* In the Gemara, the headstone is referred to as *Nefesh*, as the soul permeates its space. *Rabbi Pinchas of Koritz, Aimrei Pinchas, Likutim, 41, p. 223.*

[4] One should study Torah in honor of the deceased. *Yevamos, 122a, Rashi*, in the name of the *Gaonim*.

[5] One should recite the Haftara in the merit of a deceased parent. *Rama, Siman 376:6.*

[6] Lighting a candle during the shiva period creates joy for the soul. *Ma'avar Yavok, Ma'amar 2, Chapter 15, p. 220.* In general, souls receive pleasure when we light candles in their memory. *Rabbeinu Bachya, Shemos, 25:31; Teshuvas Torah Lishmah, Siman 520.* There is an established custom to light a candle every year on the date of a person's passing. *Maharshal, Siman 46; Magen Avraham, Siman 261:6; Nachalas Shiva, Siman 73; Mishnah Berurah, Hilchos Shabbas, 261:16.*

[7] *Gehenom* is experienced for, at most, twelve months. *Mishnah, Ediyos, 2:10*, and this is when the entire year unfolds and no zodiac influence

can find merit for the soul. *Tagmulei HaNefesh 11, p.31a; Shabbos, 33b; Zohar 1, p.107b.* Some sources say that some souls must remain in Gehenom for a longer time. *Rosh Hashanah, 17a; Baba Metzia, 58b; Zohar II, p.150b; Zohar III, p. 220b.* However, after their extended period of cleansing, they too will enter Gan Eden. *Midrash Talpiyos, Os 8, p.670.* Gehenom is viewed as a sponge, which removes negativity *Emek HaMelech, Shar Tikkunei Ha'Teshuvah, 1, p.15b.* This is also the purpose of Teshuvah *Baba Metziah 58b, Tosefos; Rosh Hashanah, 17a.* After an appropriate cleansing process, souls enter Gan Eden. *Midrash Rabbah, Shemos, 7;4. Psikta Rabbati, 53:2.* Ultimately, Gehenom itself (the experience of one's own negativity) will become null and rendered obsolete, and all souls will transcend the need for it. *Asarah Muumoros, Maamor Chikur Din, p.302. Emek HaMelech, Shar Tikkunei HaTeshuvah, 3, p.17.*

[8] Kaddish is recited in Aramaic, the ancient language that all the Jews spoke during the period after the destruction of the Temple, so that everyone could understand. *Tosefos, Berachos, 3a. Kol Bo, 7. Shibolei HaLeket, Siman 8.* And that the Angels could not understand. *Tur, Siman, 58,* so there will be no Kitrug/ negative adversary. *Bach, ad loc.*

[9] The Gemara also mentions, in a story, the importance of praying for the deceased, and specifically reciting the Kaddish. *Kallah Rabsi, 2; Midrash Tanchumah, Noach; Ohr Zaruah, 2:50.*

[10] The Name Shalom is the Yud-Hei-Vav-Hei "knocking on" Adonoi. *Agra D'Pirka, Remez 22.*

[11] The idea of Amein is to draw down from the highest to the lowest, thus, the letters that make up the word Amein (Aleph, Mem, Nun) correspond with, Aleph(1) = Kesser
        Mem (4) = Chochmah, Bina, Da'as/Chesed and Da'as/Gevurah
        Nun (5) = Tiferes, Netzach, Hod, Yesod and Malchus.
Rabbi Moshe Dovid Vally, Sefer Halikutim 2; p.480

ABOUT THE AUTHOR

RAV DOVBER PINSON

Rav DovBer Pinson is a world-renowned scholar, prolific author, thinker, and beloved spiritual teacher and mentor. Through his books, lectures and seminars he has touched and inspired the lives of thousands worldwide. Rabbi Pinson is the Rosh Yeshiva of the IYYUN Yeshiva and heads IYYUN Center in Brownstone Brooklyn.

www.IYYUN.com

OTHER BOOKS BY RAV DOVBER PINSON

Rav Pinson's books are available in all fine book stores and on the web.

REINCARNATION AND JUDAISM:
The Journey of the Soul

INNER RHYTHMS:
The Kabbalah of Music.

MEDITATION AND JUDAISM:
Exploring the Jewish Meditative Paths.

TOWARD THE INFINITE:
The Way of Kabbalistic Meditation.

JEWISH WISDOM OF THE AFTERLIFE:
The Myths, the Mysteries & Meanings

UPSHERIN:
Exploring the Laws, Customs & Meanings of a Boy's First Haircut

THIRTY-TWO GATES OF WISDOM:
Awakening through Kabbalah:

EIGHT LIGHTS: *8 Meditations for Chanukah*

RECLAIMING THE SELF: *The Pathway of Teshuvah*

נגדל ויתהדר
דהוא עתיד לאתחדתא
לאסקא לחיי עלמא ולמב[נה]
די־ירושלם ולשכלל היכלי[ה]
ולמעקר פולחנא נוכר[אה]
ולאתבא פולחנא
קודשא בריך
בחייכון וביומיכון וב
ראל בעגלא ובזמן ק[ריב]
לאתחדתא בה
עלמא ולמבני קרתא
לשכלל היכליה בגוה
ר פולחנא נוכראה מארעא

www.ingramcontent.com/pod-product-compliance
Lightning Source LLC
Chambersburg PA
CBHW071802040426
42446CB00012B/2673